The ancient monuments of
Orkney

Anna Ritchie and Graham Ritchie

Edited by Patrick Ashmore

EDINBURGH: HMSO

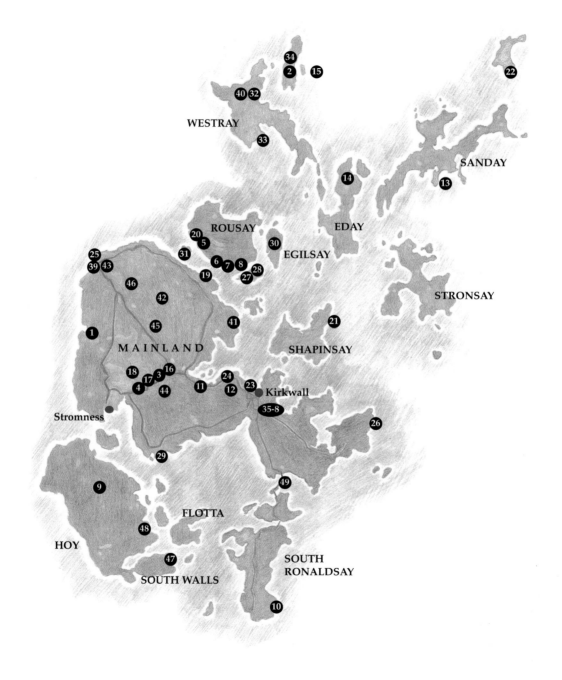

Map of Orkney showing the location of monuments in the care of the State and of Orkney Islands Council (OIC).

1 Skara Brae
2 Knap of Howar
3 Barnhouse (OIC)
4 Unstan
5 Midhowe Tomb
6 Knowe of Yarso
7 Blackhammer
8 Taversoe Tuick
9 Dwarfie Stane
10 Isbister (OIC)
11 Cuween Hill
12 Wideford Hill
13 Quoyness
14 Vinquoy (OIC)
15 Holm of Papa Westray
16 Maes Howe
17 Stones of Stenness
18 Ring of Brodgar
19 Gurness
20 Midhowe Broch
21 Burroughston (OIC)
22 Burrian (OIC access agreement)
23 Grain
24 Rennibister
25 Brough of Birsay

26 Brough of Deerness (OIC)
27 Cubbie Roo's Castle
28 St Mary's Church
29 Orphir
30 St Magnus Church
31 Eynhallow
32 Pierowall Church
33 Westside Church
34 St Boniface Church (OIC)
35 St Magnus Cathedral (OIC)
36 Bishop's Palace
37 Earl's Palace, Kirkwall
38 Tankerness House Museum (OIC)
39 Earl's Palace, Birsay
40 Noltland Castle
41 Rendall Dovecote (OIC)
42 Click Mill
43 Boardhouse Mill (OIC)
44 Tormiston Mill
45 Corrigall (OIC)
46 Kirbuster (OIC)
47 Martello Tower, Hackness
48 Scapa Flow Visitor Centre, Lyness (OIC)
49 Churchill Barriers and Italian Chapel (OIC)

All distances given in the gazetteers are travel distances, rather than as the crow flies

Contents

Until the exploits of the Vikings drew attention to northern lands, the Orkney islands were virtually on the edge of the known world. They lay far from the centres of innovation and technological progress throughout the prehistoric and early historic periods, but their inhabitants were rarely slow to develop new skills or to adopt new ideas. The fact that so many exceptional monuments survive in Orkney is no mere accident of preservation. It is true that the land has not suffered from the high degree of destruction caused by urban and industrial development or by deep ploughing and forestry that have affected other areas of Scotland; the main threat here is marine erosion. But what is remarkable about Orkney is not simply that a great number of monuments has survived, but that so many of them are in themselves outstanding human achievements.

There are about 90 islands in the Orkney archipelago, mostly formed by rocks of Middle Old Red Sandstone age, apart from the hills of Hoy which consist of Upper Old Red Sandstone rocks. There are thus plenty of good sandstones and flagstones for building purposes and, because they split easily along clear bedding planes, they present little difficulty in quarrying. It was this abundance of good stone that led to the development of a tradition of fine dry-stone building early in the prehistoric settlement of Orkney. The landscape is typical of that produced by Old Red Sandstone, predominantly gentle and rounded, but rising to spectacularly sculpted cliffs along the west and north coasts. As a place to live Orkney would have appeared very attractive to early settlers with domesticated animals. Although not quite as bare of trees as today, the islands were unencumbered by the dense forest-cover which made so much of mainland Scotland difficult for early farmers to clear. Light woodlands of alder, birch and willow grew in hollows where there was some shelter from the wind; otherwise the open grasslands were ideal for grazing.

Scattered throughout the mainland of Orkney and the islands is a remarkable range of well-preserved monuments illustrating every major phase of building achievement over past centuries; the examples now in the care of Historic Scotland reflect many aspects of Orcadian history, from the wartime importance of Scapa Flow anchorages in the nineteenth and twentieth centuries, underlined by the martello towers of Hoy, to the once familiar water-mills essential to the daily bread of a farming people. The political turbulence and wealth of the times is graphically portrayed by the grim castle of Noltland and the splendour of the Earl's Palaces of Birsay and Kirkwall. Spiritual and communal life is represented over a long period from an unusual variety of early medieval churches to the great stone circles of remote prehistory, and Orkney is particularly fortunate in the number and quality of early stone-built tombs open to the public. All too often, it is the everyday, domestic aspects of the past that remain obscure, but here the abundance of good building stone has ensured the survival not just of the State monuments of great men but also of the homes of ordinary people: the hall-houses of Norse settlers on the Brough of Birsay, the massed housing of Iron-Age villagers round the chieftain's broch at Gurness, the dwellings and workshops of early farmers at Skara Brae and Knap of Howar.

In addition to those in State care, comparable monuments are included here which are owned by or in the care of Orkney Islands Council, or where access has been agreed with the owner. Among them, the early houses at Barnhouse give a glimpse of the complex society using the ceremonial Stones of Stenness, while the so-called 'Tomb of the Eagles' at Isbister enhances our perception of burial practices. A fine broch at Burroughston is surrounded by a particularly well-preserved rampart. St Magnus Cathedral is a remarkable achievement which

The ceremonial circle of Ring of Brodgar

began in Orkney's Golden Age of the twelfth century. Rural life of recent times is illustrated by two farm museums, Corrigall and Kirbuster, and the famous Italian Chapel is a fitting reminder of Orkney's role in World War II. Lyness and the Churchill Barriers underline the strategic naval importance of Scapa Flow.

For the period before written records, dating depends upon scientific methods of analysis, particularly radiocarbon analysis carried out on organic materials such as bone and charcoal. Orcadian prehistory is supported by a good number of radiocarbon dates and they are the basis for the dates used in this book.

There was such a lot of archaeological excavation in Orkney in the 1970s and 1980s that the islands have come to dominate understanding of aspects of the prehistory of Scotland, but of course Scotland's landscape is diverse and the way in which people exploited it has varied accordingly. Compared with other areas of Scotland, our knowledge of Orkney's past is rich and exciting – but the picture is still fragmented and there is much yet to discover.

Before farming was introduced into Scotland, people lived by hunting, fishing and gathering wild foodstuffs. They tended not to live permanently in one place but to move about in search of a livelihood, perhaps returning to the same places at certain times of the year. Orkney was surely known to these people, but as yet there are only a few flint tools to prove it. Coastal erosion has destroyed many ancient sites, and among them may have been traces of some of the earliest pioneering colonists.

Small communities of farmers began to settle in the islands before the middle of the fourth millennium BC. They brought with them the cattle and sheep that formed their stock and seed-corn for their first harvests. The skills of stock-rearing and agriculture are of European and ultimately Near Eastern origin, but the first permanent Orcadian residents were related to communities in Caithness and along the Atlantic seaways of western Scotland, rather than immigrants direct from the continent.

The way of life of these farming peoples can be glimpsed from the remains of their houses, burial places and ceremonial monuments and from the material recovered from archaeological excavation, such as pottery, flint and animal bones. Two settlements are in State care at Skara Brae and Knap of Howar, together with Barnhouse in the care of Orkney Islands Council, but others are known from excavation at a number of places, including Rinyo in Rousay, Links of Noltland in Westray and Pool in Sanday.

On the shore of Bay of Skaill on the west coast of the mainland of Orkney is one of the most remarkable monuments in Britain. There are the houses and alleyways of a small village which was flourishing on the edge of the then known world around 5000 years ago. And it is not just foundations that survive; in some cases the walls of the houses stand to eaves level and alleyways are still roofed over with the original stone slabs. During its lifetime, the settlement became embedded in its own rubbish heaps and, after it was abandoned, it became

*Five thousand year-old houses preserved
at Skara Brae*

choked with sand. The combination of refuse and sand has preserved the buildings and debris of everyday life to a unique degree and, because timber was scarce and good stone available, even the furniture inside the houses was built in stone and still survives.

Not surprisingly, Skara Brae has attracted a good deal of attention since its discovery around 1850, for it gives a vivid insight into the daily life of an early farming community. It is clear that people were living here continuously over several generations, dismantling old dwellings and building new ones as the need arose. Their tool kit remained much the same throughout; the last inhabitants had been using essentially the same sort of pottery vessels as their ancestors who founded the settlement. The maximum number of houses at any one period seems to have been between six and eight and it is probable that there were no more than 40 to 50 people in the community.

One of the most striking aspects of the village is that the houses look as if they were all built to the same design. Each consists of a large square room, with a central fireplace, a bed on either side and a shelved dresser against the wall opposite the doorway. On closer inspection there are some differences; in the older houses the beds are set into the thickness of the wall, and one house on the edge of the village is quite different. This oval building (no. 8) appears to have been a workshop rather than a dwelling. When it was first uncovered, there were hundreds of stone chips on the floor, suggesting that stone tools had been made here. The shape of this workshop is similar to that of contemporary buildings in Shetland. Traces of other oval or round houses have been found by excavation at Skara Brae, reinforcing the idea that there may once have been a greater variety of buildings than now survives.

All the same, there is a distinctive 'Skara Brae type' of house which was also built at Rinyo and at Barnhouse. Was it simply a fashion or could it have had some deeper meaning?

Whatever the reason for the architectural design, this would have been a comfortable, warm and spacious family dwelling. The beds would have had 'mattresses' of straw or heather and coverings of soft sheepskin or deerskin. Displayed on the dresser may have

Digging at Skara Brae in 1972

Decorated slab from a bed in House 7

been ceremonial carved stone balls and pottery jars full of preserved food or drink or the precious seed for next year's crops. Deep slab-boxes were set into the floor, their corners carefully sealed with clay in order to hold liquid, perhaps to soak limpets for fish-bait. Small cells built into the thickness of the house wall gave extra storage space. The door into the communal passage could be barred against intruders – the door itself may have been a thin flagstone or made of stiffened hide on a wooden frame, but the holes on either side for the wooden bar still survive.

The type of pottery used at Skara Brae is now known as Grooved Ware: large flat-bottomed vessels sometimes highly decorated with moulded rims, with pellets or spirals of clay stuck to the outside of the pot or designs cut into the surface of the clay before firing.

The inhabitants were settled farmers, as animal bones (cattle, sheep) and grains of cultivated cereal prove, but they were also fishermen and at least occasionally hunters as well. Flint was used for implements which needed sharp edges, such as scrapers for preparing animal skins, leaf-shaped points and simple knives, and large beach pebbles were collected and used as hammers and pounders. Bone awls could be used for making holes in leather in order to fashion clothes – weaving was unknown in Scotland at this period. Elegant bone pins were used to fasten clothing, and beads and pendants were worn as necklaces.

Artefacts comparable to those discovered at Skara Brae have been found not only at other settlements but also at two other types of site – chambered tombs such as that at Quoyness on the island of Sanday and the stone circle known as the Stones of Stenness. Grooved Ware is also found elsewhere in Scotland and in south and east England, underlining the fact that Orkney had far-ranging contacts at this time. The pottery was made locally in a widely fashionable style, but other materials might be imported, such as the pitchstone from Arran in western Scotland that was used at Barnhouse.

Established somewhat earlier than Skara Brae was the farmstead at Knap of Howar in Papa Westray. Here the houses are oblong rather than square, and, although they have built-in shelves and cupboards and a stone bench, there are no storage cells, limpet boxes, dressers or beds as at Skara Brae. The economic base was the same, with mixed farming, fishing and hunting, and much of the ordinary domestic equipment was the same, but the pottery was quite different. The people at Knap of Howar made round-based bowls and jars in a style known as Unstan Ware; the finest bowls were small and delicately decorated.

This type of pottery is named after the tomb at Unstan, where some 30 broken bowls were found, and its use with burials seems to have been confined to tombs of one particular design. These stalled cairns resemble the houses at Knap of Howar, at present the only settlement in Orkney to have yielded Unstan Ware in any quantity.

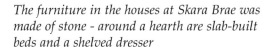

The furniture in the houses at Skara Brae was made of stone - around a hearth are slab-built beds and a shelved dresser

Places to visit:

1. Skara Brae, Mainland

Located 10.2 km N of Stromness (A967 and B9056) and about 25.5 km NW of Kirkwall (A965 and B9055); carpark; site museum and guidebook. OS 1:50 000 map sheet 6; HY 231187.

A pleasant walk across the links of Bay of Skaill is rewarded by an astonishing glimpse into the life of a community flourishing for some 500 years from about 3000 BC. The latest houses are the best-preserved, with their stone furnishings, and passages wind between them. Do not miss the faintly carved stones protected by glass sheets.

2. Knap of Howar, Papa Westray

Located on the W coast of the island of Papa Westray, 800 m W of Holland House. OS 1:50 000 map sheet 5; HY 483518.

Here two well-built houses were preserved beneath a blanket of windblown sand. They are the visible remains of a small farm that flourished between about 3500 and 2800 BC. The larger house was divided into two rooms by a partition of slabs and timber posts, and wood or whale ribs must also have played a part in roofing the house. The hearth, no longer visible, was simply a shallow pit in the innermost room, and there may have been wooden benches lining the walls. Two quernstones can still be seen, used for grinding grain and also for crushing shells which were mixed into the clay for making pottery. The outer room has a stone platform along one wall. The smaller building was

The smaller bulding at Knap of Howar with the passage leading into the dwelling-house alongside

divided into three rooms, with a stone hearth in the central room and shelves and cupboards built into the walls.

The inhabitants reared cattle, sheep and pigs and grew grain. But they did not scorn the natural resources of the island; they hunted deer, fished and gathered a variety of shellfish such as oysters, limpets, scallops, whelks and razor-shells. They made their own pottery in the Unstan Ware style, as well as making tools of stone, flint and bone – including a spatula or flat spoon like those which are still familiar pieces of kitchen equipment today.

The people at Knap of Howar may have used the stalled cairn at the north end of the Holm of Papa Westray for their burials.

3. Barnhouse, Mainland (Orkney Islands Council)

Beside the Loch of Harray, just beyond the Stones of Stenness, on the E side of the B9055, to the N of its junction with the Kirkwall to Stromness road (A965). OS 1:50 000 map sheet 6; HY 307127.

Only the foundations survived of the houses here, and the base of the walls have been rebuilt in new stone. They echo those at Skara Brae in their design, with beds recessed into the walls. Two are more elaborate versions, in one case a double house and in the other an unusually large house, or hall, set on a low platform. Aspects of their design show a close relationship with nearby Maes Howe, and their hearths are very similar to the central setting at the Stones of Stenness, underlining the part that ritual played in all spheres of life and death. All the houses had stone-built drains leading to ditches which ran into the loch. Some of the houses had been demolished and rebuilt several times over four centuries from about 3200 BC.

A reconstructed house with the large building in the background

Houses of the dead

Burial and ritual monuments of the fourth and third millennia BC are well represented in Orkney. Chambered tombs were burial-vaults built to receive interments over a long period, and they may well have been the focus for other forms of ritual or worship which the techniques of archaeology cannot detect. In most cases, the tomb was sited in a prominent position on the margin of the best land, within easy walking distance of the local community. There are no fewer than 15 tombs in the island of Rousay, and their spacing relates very clearly to individual units of land. The sites of settlements are known on the lower slopes of the hillsides on which the tombs of Cuween and Wideford are set. It is estimated that the average tomb took between 1000 and 10 000 man-hours to build, according to its size, and the task may have been achieved by co-operation between several communities. More difficult to estimate is whether such monuments housed the dead of the whole community or of an élite ruling class.

Most tombs were built with their entrances facing approximately south-east, probably towards the midwinter sunrise – the time of year when the brief winter days begin to lengthen and thoughts turn to spring. An exception is Maes Howe, where the passage faces south-west and the setting sun at midwinter shines down the passage and into the chamber.

There are two main types of tomb in Orkney. The first is part of a group known as Orkney-Cromarty tombs, which is widely distributed in north and west Scotland; it includes the stalled cairns of Orkney. The second type is named after Maes Howe and is unique to Orkney.

The Orcadian stalled cairns are characterised by rectangular chambers set within either circular or roughly rectangular cairns – the chambers are subdivided by pairs of upright slabs into individual compartments or burial-lairs. At both Knowe of Yarso and Midhowe the passage and chamber are on the same axis, but at another group of sites (Blackhammer, Unstan and Isbister) the passage is at right angles to the chamber.

Inside the Tomb at Maes Howe

The discovery of skeletal remains, pottery and flint is more difficult to interpret as it is likely that the chambers were used to receive burials over a long period and thus the chambers or sections of them may have been cleared out in order to make room for further burials. It follows, therefore, that what is recovered in the course of an excavation are the burial deposits present when the tomb was sealed permanently or went out of use – perhaps with the extinction of a family line.

A clear picture of the contents of the tomb at the time of closure comes from Midhowe, where 25 individuals were found; where still intact they were crouched burials, but in other cases the bones had been gathered together to form a heap in the centre of the compartment. At Knowe of Yarso, where there were the remains of 29 interments, earlier burials had been neatly re-arranged, with skulls placed in rows along the walls of the innermost compartment. The remains of more than 300 people were found in the tomb at Isbister, but many of them were represented by only a few bones. This treatment of ancestral bones suggests that people believed that the spirit or soul was released when the body decayed rather than at the moment of death. Once the corpses had been reduced to bones, they could safely be pushed aside to make room for new burials.

At Isbister, the carcasses of sea-eagles had been placed deliberately in the chamber, hinting perhaps at totemic ideas – hence the site has become known as 'The Tomb of the Eagles'. The 24 dog skulls in the Cuween Hill tomb may also represent a tribal emblem, or perhaps an offering to the gods to ensure good hunting.

Human skulls in a side cell at Isbister

Although pottery, flints and other objects were placed in the tombs, they were not grave-goods in the sense of belonging to any particular skeleton and may simply have been involved in the rites surrounding the burials.

A sub-group of the Orkney-Cromarty tombs, sometimes known as the Bookan type, is characterised by oval or rectangular chambers subdivided into compartments by upright slabs projecting radially from the side walls. The lower chamber and the miniature chamber of Taversoe Tuick are examples of this type and both have involved cutting into the rock in order to hollow out the space for the chamber. Such engineering expertise would also have been essential for the careful cutting of the chamber and passage for the other example of this group – the Dwarfie Stane on the island of Hoy. This rock-cut tomb in its bleak setting evokes the religious fervour of the early inhabitants of Orkney.

The other main type of chambered tomb is named after the magnificent Maes Howe. Of the ten or eleven examples of this type, no less than five are in State care (Maes Howe, Cuween Hill, Wideford Hill, Quoyness and Holm of Papa Westray South) and one in the care of Orkney Islands Council (Vinquoy). At Maes Howe itself, a central chamber is entered by a long passage leading in from the edge of the mound, and there is a small cell opening off each of the other three walls of the chamber. The tombs on Cuween Hill and Wideford Hill are very similar to Maes Howe, but at Vinquoy the design is less regular and there are four side-cells. At Quoyness and Holm of Papa Westray South the basic plan has been elaborated by the addition of more cells, and this has resulted in the elongation of the central chamber.

Just as the design of stalled tombs echoed that of the houses at Knap of Howar, Maes Howe tombs resemble the houses at Skara Brae and similar settlements. People clearly liked the idea of houses of the dead. The main difference was that the burial chambers were roofed with stone slabs and covered with a cairn of stones or clay and stones. The entrance passage into a tomb was much longer and often lower than that into a domestic house.

Burials were found at Cuween Hill and Quoyness but do not appear to have survived at the other sites. Quoyness also contained pottery, spiked stone objects and a large bone pin with a knob on one side. The stone objects (which have been interpreted as ceremonial maceheads) and the bone pin are closely similar to finds from Skara Brae.

Tombs seem to have been an essential part of the life of the early farmers from the start of their colonisation of Orkney. The earliest radiocarbon dates come from stalled cairns at Point of Cott in Westray and Isbister and from the Maes Howe-type tomb at Quanterness, near Kirkwall, and they suggest that these tombs were built in the period 3500–3000 BC. Individual tombs were clearly used over several centuries, and the custom of burying in these tombs seems to have continued until about 2500 BC. The end of the life of a tomb was marked either by sealing the entrance passage or by removing the roof and filling both the chamber and the entrance passage with earth and stones.

An exciting discovery in recent years was in a large rock-cut pit at Sand Fiold at the north end of the Bay of Skaill, within sight of Skara Brae. The pit contained a large box built of flagstones, one side of which was ingeniously 'hinged' to allow easy access. The design is very different from conventional tombs, apart from the idea of access for successive burials, yet it was first constructed early in the third millennium and was therefore contemporary with many tombs. It warns us that our perception of burial practices may be biased by what has survived so spectacularly above ground-level.

Men, women and children of all ages were buried in chambered tombs. As a result of analysis of the many human bones found at Isbister and Quanterness, a picture has emerged of a population in which few people reached the age of 50 years and most, if they survived childhood, died in their twenties. It is a surprisingly gloomy picture, given the advantages of a good climate and ample food resources.

Places to visit:

Few chambered tombs have their original roofs intact but the modern concrete domes are easily recognisable. There is no access for wheelchairs at most sites.

4. Unstan, Mainland

Located about 4 km NE of Stromness on the Kirkwall road (A965). OS 1:50 000 map sheet 6; HY 282117.

The builders chose a promontory of land projecting into the Loch of Stenness. An oval cairn covers a stalled chamber with two end-compartments that appear each to have been divided horizontally by means of a slab-shelf, although only the supporting stones bonded into the side walls survive. In the centre of the W wall is the entrance to a small side-cell; some Norse runes and a bird are carved on the lintel-stone above the entrance, but the stone is not in its original position.

The tomb was excavated in 1884 and is remarkable for the number of Unstan Ware bowls that were recovered (at least 30); four leaf-shaped arrowheads and a finely made flint implement were also recorded. Human bones were found in each compartment and two crouched skeletons were discovered in the side-cell.

At Unstan, a low opening on the right of the chamber leads into a small cell

5. Midhowe Chambered Tomb, Rousay

Located on the W coast of the island close to Midhowe Broch; signposted path. OS 1:50 000 map sheet 6; HY 372304. On the Westness Walk, which includes other chambered tombs, brochs, and Norse and later remains.

After excavation in the 1930s, this large stalled cairn was protected by a vast shed, with the result that all the details of the cairn's construction can be seen. The central chamber is fully 23 m long and almost complete, and the entrance passage is still blocked by original walling. The outer face of the cairn was carefully built on a foundation course of flat horizontal slabs; above this the slabs are set at an angle and in the next layer the slabs are laid in the opposite direction to those beneath. The resultant herring-bone pattern is best seen on the E wall.

There are 12 compartments in the chamber, and the end-compartment is further subdivided by slabs and may have had a shelf at a height of about 1 m above floor level. The chamber walls are still 2.5 m high and were originally higher – this long gallery must

Looking down the long burial chamber at Midhowe

have been a particularly dark and awe-inspiring vault. In several compartments the burials were placed on or under low stone benches: skeletons were discovered between the fifth and the tenth compartments (counting from the entrance), generally in a crouched position with their back against the NE wall of the chamber. Some pottery was recovered from the seventh compartment on the SW side of the chamber. The chamber had been deliberately filled with stones when it went out of use, and two later crouched burials were discovered in the filling itself (one in a stone cist).

6. Knowe of Yarso, Rousay

Located on the S coast of the island, 500 m NNE of the public road (B9064); a steep climb up a signposted path. OS 1:50 000 map sheet 6; HY 404279.

The cairn is rectangular with rounded ends, and the stones of its outer face were laid in slanting courses, a decorative technique which can still be seen on either side of the entrance. Note the vertical break in the wall on either side of the passage about 1.2 m from the outside, which marks the line of the inner revetment within the cairn.

The interior of the tomb is well-preserved, with three compartments divided by upright slabs; the inner compartment is twice the size of the other two, but low slabs mark an end-compartment which was probably furnished with a shelf (a ledge survives in the NE wall).

Excavation in 1934 revealed the remains of at least 29 individuals, the majority found in the innermost compartment; 17 were represented only by skulls and 15 of these were placed side by side at the bottom of the wall with their faces turned inwards. There were also bones from at least 36 red deer, scattered throughout the burial deposits and the filling of the chamber and passage. A single radiocarbon date indicates that the tomb was in use about 2900 BC.

7. Blackhammer, Rousay

Located on the S coast of the island of Rousay, N of the public road (B9064); signposted path. OS 1:50 000 map sheet 6; HY 414276.

The cairn covering the burial chamber is oblong, and its outer face was originally built with a decorative design of slanting slabs in broad interlocking triangles. The entrance passage was sealed when the cairn was abandoned, and access is now by way of a ladder through the modern roof.

The chamber was divided by pairs of upright flagstones into seven compartments, but the masonry in the centre of the chamber was built later than the construction of the tomb, and the four missing uprights may have been demolished at the same time.

Two skeletons were found during the excavation, one in the entrance passage and the other in the westernmost compartment; in a hollow in the floor of the adjoining compartment were found the remains of an Unstan bowl and a burnt flint knife. Other objects discovered in the chamber include a stone axe and several flint tools.

The burial chamber at Blackhammer is covered by a modern roof

8. Taversoe Tuick, Rousay

Located on the S coast of the island, 200 m W of Trumland, N of the public road (B9064); signposted path. OS 1:50 000 map sheet 6; HY 425276.

The chambered tomb of Taversoe Tuick is an unusual monument, with two chambers set one above the other. The lower chamber was dug into the hillside and was originally entered by a passage on the SE side; it is roughly rectangular and divided into four compartments. All are provided with shelves, on which skeletal remains, including a crouched burial, were discovered. Three piles of cremated bones had been deposited in the passage. The upper chamber is entered by a passage from the N side and is completely enclosed by a modern dome. The central chamber of the upper tomb is divided into two – a small compartment at the NE end, entered between two upright slabs, and the main chamber which is divided into two compartments.

Three stone cists or coffins were built at some later date in the main chamber, but these have been removed during excavation; they contained the cremated remains of several adults and a child. A miniature tomb was dug into the ground outside the cairn; it has a pear-shaped chamber divided by four upright slabs, and the lintelled roof is still intact. Three almost complete pottery bowls were found in the chamber but no burial remains survived. The entrance is now protected by a wooden hatch.

9. The Dwarfie Stane, Hoy

Located about 4 km from the landing place at Moaness in the N part of the island; signposted. OS 1:50 000 map sheet 6; HY 243004.

A dramatically steep valley runs across the island between Quoys and Rackwick, and the Dwarfie Stane on its terrace commands wide views across to mainland Orkney over Scapa Flow. This great block of red sandstone is 8.5 m long, up to 4.5 m wide and 2 m high, perfect for a small rock-cut tomb.

The Dwarfie Stone on its remote hillside

A short passage was cut into the west face of the stone, and the large block that now lies outside the entrance was clearly designed to seal it. The passage leads into a square chamber with a slightly higher roof and a cell on either side. The cells are divided from the central area by distinct kerbs forming carefully squared doorways into the rounded cells.

The entrance was certainly blocked in the sixteenth century, and it may be that the breach in the roof of the chamber was caused during an attempt to break into the tomb, but this hole has now been skilfully restored.

This is a remarkable monument because of its situation, careful construction and its part in recent folklore; Norna of Fitful Head in Sir Walter Scott's novel, *The Pirate*, describes 'this extraordinary dwelling, which Trolld, a dwarf famous in the northern Sagas, is said to have framed for his own favourite residence'.

Among the many names carved on the stone, look for the inscription in beautiful Persian letters. It reads 'I have sat two nights and so learnt patience', and it was carved by Major W Mouncey in 1850, who also carved the date and his name backwards in Latin.

10. Isbister, South Ronaldsay (Orkney Islands Council)

Located on the SE coast of the island, beyond Liddle Farm; from the end of the A961 from Kirkwall, take the B9041 and then the signposted side-road southwards. OS 1:50 000 map sheet 7; ND 470845. Finds in Tankerness House Museum.

The chamber of this important stalled cairn was excavated in the 1970s. The original roof had been removed when the tomb went out of use and was filled with earth and stones around 2500 BC. The entrance faces E, out to sea, while from inland the cairn must always have been very prominent on the skyline.

Within an oval cairn, the passage enters the chamber at right angles, as at Unstan (no. 4); whereas Unstan has one side-cell, Isbister has three, and the main chamber is divided into three compartments with a shelved end-compartment extending its length at either end to 8 m. The two cells on the west side of the chamber held many skulls as well as other human bones, and there were human, animal and fish bones throughout the chamber (the third side-cell had been robbed before the excavation), together with many broken Unstan Ware bowls.

The tomb had been built sometime before 3000 BC and was used over a long period of perhaps 700 years. Not surprisingly, it contained bones from a large number of people – at least 338 – although many individuals were represented by only a few bones. There was also an unexpected number of bones and talons of sea-eagles, perhaps a tribal emblem.

11. Cuween Hill, Mainland

Located about 1.2 km SSE of Finstown, signposted from the A965 Kirkwall to Finstown road. OS 1:50 000 map sheet 6; HY 363127.

This cairn lies on the flank of Cuween Hill with extensive views across the Bay of Firth. The tomb is entered along a narrow passage, 5.5 m long, the outer part of which is unroofed but the inner part is roofed with slabs at a height of only 0.8 m. This passage is more difficult to negotiate than most other Orkney tombs, but the high quality of the interior masonry makes it a particularly interesting example (a torch is helpful).

The Maes Howe-type chamber is roughly rectangular and the walls still stand to a height of 2.3 m (the roof is modern). The lower parts of the walls are vertical, but the upper courses oversail slightly as they rise. There are four side-cells, one of them a double cell, entered through small openings. There were the remains of eight skeletons, five skulls on the floor of the main chamber and others in the S and W compartments and at the end of the chamber. A large quantity of animal bones was also recovered, including an extraordinary, and surely totemic, deposit of 24 dog skulls on the floor of the chamber.

Now empty, the chamber and cells at Cuween once held human and animal bones

12. Wideford Hill, Mainland

Located 4 km W of Kirkwall on the W slope of Wideford Hill, the path to the tomb starts by the masts on Wideford Hill, c 4km W of Kirkwall, and runs 0.5km over rough moorland OS 1:50 000 map sheet 6; HY 409121.

This Maes Howe-type tomb was built in a commanding situation below the crest of Wideford Hill, with a superb view across the Bay of Firth. The circular cairn has a carefully constructed outer face and two inner revetment walls can be seen as a result of excavation, although originally they may not have been visible.

The entrance faces W over the fertile lands below, and the passage is extremely low and narrow (a trapdoor and ladder now provide access to the tomb). There is a well-built rectangular chamber and the oversailing masonry and the large lintel-stones over the cells and passage demonstrate considerable architectural expertise.

The entrance to the tomb on Wideford Hill

13. Quoyness, Sanday

Located on the E side of the peninsula known as Els Ness on the S coast of the island; it is about 4 km from the airstrip. OS 1:50 000 map sheet 5; HY 676378.

The external appearance of this spectacular tomb is confusing, displaying as it does the complex structure of the cairn rather than its original appearance. The mound stands on an irregular platform and survives to a height of more than 4 m. The outer face of the mound, which is continuous in front of the entrance, may be connected with the final blocking of the tomb rather than with its use as a monument for collective burial.

A long entrance passage leads into a spacious burial chamber of Maes Howe-type; the walls rise vertically for 1 m and then oversail to reduce the final span to be roofed at a height of about 4 m. When the cairn was excavated, two features were found in the floor of the main chamber: a circular stone-lined cist in the S corner and an oval depression in the NE corner. The cist contained the partial remains of at least ten adults and four or five children, but there were no skeletal remains in the oval depression.

Six irregular cells are entered from the main chamber, and skulls and bones were found in all but two of them (the two in the opposite wall from the passage). Excavation also produced a polished bone pin with a projection on one side and a polished slate object, shaped rather like a hammer head, both of which can be paralleled among the finds from Skara Brae. Radiocarbon analysis of human bones suggests that the tomb was in use around 2900 BC.

14. Vinquoy, Eday (Orkney Islands Council)

Located on Vinquoy Hill at the N end of the island; signposted from the B9063; heritage trail leaflet. OS 1:50 000 map sheet 5; HY 560381. On the Eday Heritage Walk.

A most conspicuous setting was chosen by the builders of this Maes Howe-type tomb; although it is not quite at the crest of the hill, on a clear day almost the whole of Orkney can be seen from here.

The tomb is built of Eday sandstone, which can be shaped and used to great effect as in St Magnus Cathedral, but which unshaped as here results in very uneven walling. This is why the tomb seems very irregular in design, although its builders were careful to use slivers of stone to achieve level roofing lintels. There are four cells opening off the main chamber, but nothing is known of their original contents. A modern clear dome has been placed over the main chamber in order to light it.

The Eday Heritage Walk takes the visitor past the great Standing Stone of Setter, the chambered tombs of Braeside and Huntersquoy, and a massive enclosure known as the Fold of Setter.

15. Holm of Papa Westray South

Located in the SE of the island of Holm of Papa Westray. OS 1:50 000 map sheet 5; HY 509518.

Holm of Papa Westray is a small island off the E side of Papa Westray, separated from it by the bay of South Wick. On the highest part of the island the long mound of the Maes Howe-type cairn is a conspicuous landmark, and near the N tip of the island there is a recently excavated stalled cairn.

The south cairn covers a wonderfully elaborate tomb, with a chamber over 20 m long and no fewer than 12 side-cells, two of which are double cells. Although the main chamber was designed to be tall and spacious, the entrance passage is long, narrow and very low and the entrances into the end-cells

Moving about in the tomb proved as difficult for the modern surveyor as for the original mourners

and side-cells are also very low. Today's visitor enters through a hatch in the roof and a ladder, but the original entry must have seemed a long slow crawl into the bowels of the earth.

On plan the layout of the central chamber and side-cells may seem at some remove from the architectural exactness of Maes Howe, but the masonry of the chamber is of a high order; the lowest 1.5 m of the side-walls is vertical, then they converge to narrow the roofing span.

An unusual feature of this tomb is the presence of a number of stones decorated by the original users of the tomb; the lintel above the SE cell is decorated with several depressions, two 'eye-brow' motifs and a symbol not unlike the letters EAU. On the opposite wall a zigzag and a series of almost circular motifs have been carved. On the SE side-wall of the main chamber, about 1.5 m S of the entrance passage and at a height of 1.4 m, there is a fractured stone with what has been a double ring and conjoined pecked circles with central dots.

16. Maes Howe, Mainland

Located about 14.5 km W of Kirkwall on the main Kirkwall to Stromness road (A965); park at Tormiston Mill (no. 44); guidebook. OS 1:50 000 map sheet 6; HY 318127.

The chambered tomb of Maes Howe is one of the greatest architectural achievements of the prehistoric peoples of Scotland; although made possible by the tractable nature of the Orkney flagstones, the conception and craftsmanship of the tomb make it a most remarkable construction.

A daunting long passage leads into the chamber at Maes Howe

On entering the fenced enclosure the visitor passes through a bank surrounding the site; the lower part of this bank has been shown by excavation to be of prehistoric date. The mound and the flattened platform on which it stands are encircled by a shallow ditch. The grass-covered barrow, 35 m in diameter and 7.3 m in height, is composed of clay and angular fragments of rock and encloses the stone-built cairn within which stands the tomb chamber itself. Radiocarbon analysis of peat from the bottom of the ditch indicates that the tomb was built sometime before 2700 BC.

The entrance passage is on the SW side of the mound; the outer part was originally almost 7m long, and about 0.7m in width and height. Some 2m in from the present entrance the passage expands to a width of about 0.9 m with a door jamb on each side. The step down is modern, leading to the original passage floor level. There are two features for the visitor to notice while negotiating the passage; the first is the recess which houses the closing stone designed to block the entrance, and the second is the method of construction of the inner part of the passage with monumental slabs. One side-slab is fully 5.6 m in length and the positioning of this and other slabs in the passage is a most impressive engineering feat.

The initial reaction of the visitor may be that the chamber is smaller than expected, for it takes a moment or two to appreciate the proportions and sense of architectural balance that the builders have achieved. The chamber is some 4.75 m square with a projecting stone buttress in each corner; one

The great mound of Maes Howe still dominates the Orkney landscape

A runic inscriptiom in Maes Howe

side of each buttress is made of a single upright slab and it is perhaps the contrast between these tall pillars and the horizontal dry-stone walls of the chamber that suggests a feeling of space. The buttresses, however, have a very practical purpose, as the walls of the chamber rise vertically for 1.37 m from the floor and then converge gradually to a height of 2.6 m, with the slanting natural fracture of the outer edges of the slabs providing an almost smooth surface. From this point to their surviving height of 3.8 m the walls converge slab by slab to form a square corbelled vault with the buttresses providing important internal support. The upper part of the roof (now painted white) has been reconstructed.

There are three side-cells, which were probably sealed by the substantial rectangular blocks that now lie in front of their entrances. Unfortunately, we have no record of burials or artefacts from this astounding tomb. It was excavated in 1861 but not for the first time – Norsemen had broken into the mound on several occasions in the twelfth century AD (one such occasion is vividly described in *Orkneyinga Saga*). On the walls of the tomb are some 30 inscriptions carved in Scandinavian runes, together with an exquisite lion.

Five of the inscriptions mention treasure – for instance, 'It is long ago that a great treasure lay hidden here'. Treasure to the Vikings meant gold or silver, but metal was unknown to the prehistoric builders of the tomb. Could the tomb have been opened and re-used in later times? Excavation has yielded evidence that the surrounding bank was rebuilt in the ninth century AD. Perhaps the tomb was re-used for the burial of a Viking chief and his treasure in the ninth century, only to be robbed by his descendants three centuries later.

If most chambered tombs represent local communal burial places, some, especially Maes Howe, must have been built to demonstrate the power of a social élite. It has been estimated that the labour required for the building of most tombs involved around 10 000 man-hours or less, but that the supreme architecture of Maes Howe would have called for some 100 000 man-hours.

This suggests that the early farming society in Orkney gradually developed into larger tribal units capable of organising the construction of major ceremonial monuments. From about 2900 BC the heartland of mainland Orkney, centred on the lochs of Stenness and Harray, blossomed into a great ceremonial meeting-place. The Stones of Stenness and the Ring of Brodgar are public monuments of a scale that Orkney had never seen before, the focus for religious or legal ritual for the islands as a whole. A short distance away is the great tomb of Maes Howe (no.16), and adjacent to the Stones of Stenness is the Barnhouse settlement (no. 3).

The twin promontories between the lochs of Stenness and Harray, now linked by the narrow bridge of Brodgar, contain two of the most evocative of the megalithic monuments of Orkney – the Stones of Stenness and the Ring of Brodgar. These stone circles are

Sunset over the Ring of Brodgar

visible from many places (one of the best views is from Staney Hill), and from the stones themselves there are panoramic views of the mainland hills and of the steep cliffs of the island of Hoy.

Henge monuments are earthwork circles comprising an inner ditch and outer bank with one or more entrance causeways. A small proportion of henges contain stone circles, as at the Stones of Stenness and the Ring of Brodgar. The Stones of Stenness is likely to be the earlier of the two monuments, dating from around 2900 BC; originally there was a circle of 12 stones set within a rock-cut ditch and outer bank. The use of this ceremonial circle was broadly contemporary with the settlements at Barnhouse and Skara Brae and with the Maes Howe-type of tomb such as Quoyness and Maes Howe itself.

Excavations in the 1970s revealed broken Grooved Ware pots in a central stone setting and also at the bottom of the ditch, along with animal bones which might suggest feasting or sacrifice. There is every reason to believe that the building of this ritual monument, involving the quarrying from the ditch of many tonnes of stone, would be a long and probably seasonal undertaking of many thousands of man-hours.

The engineering feat achieved by the building of the Ring of Brodgar was even greater – a larger amount of stone was removed from the ditch and the 60 standing stones were positioned on an uneven site with considerable accuracy. No excavation has been carried out within the stones and our information about the nearby barrows is equally slight.

It has been suggested that the circle and the mounds round about it form a lunar observatory from which variations in the moon's movements could be examined from three positions. The date at which the barrows could have been used in this way has been calculated to be about 1560 BC in calendar years. It is, however, likely that the construction of the circle was considerably earlier than this and, without excavation, the date of the barrows cannot be determined. There was certainly an interest in the movements of the sun and moon, as the alignment of the passage into Maes Howe demonstrates very clearly; around midwinter sunset, the rays of the sun penetrate down the passage and into the chamber.

This ceremonial centre remained important to the people of Orkney for almost 2000 years. Only a small number of monuments of this period are in State care – the barrows, or earthen burial-mounds, at Brodgar and some of the isolated standing stones. A new burial ritual was introduced after 2000 BC involving individual interment in a small stone coffin or cist within an earthen mound or cairn. At least five such cists have been

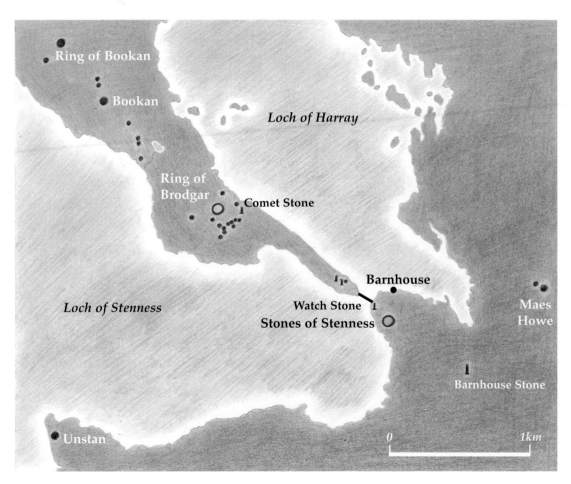

Ring of Bookan

Bookan

Loch of Harray

Ring of Brodgar

Comet Stone

Loch of Stenness

Barnhouse

Watch Stone

Stones of Stenness

Maes Howe

Barnhouse Stone

Unstan

0   1km

found on the Ness of Brodgar, four of them lying parallel to one another in a line running north and south; overlapping two of the cists was a slab decorated with lozenges, chevrons and other linear motifs.

On the south-east of the Ring of Brodgar there are numerous small mounds but, although some of them appear to have been excavated in the past, nothing is known about their contents. There are two more impressive mounds, one on the south lip of the henge ditch and the other, known as Salt Knowe, situated 100 m south-west of the henge. A cist has been revealed in Salt Knowe, but neither mound has been fully excavated. To the east of the Ring of Brodgar stands the Comet Stone on a low platform with the stumps of two other stones. Close to the shore of the Loch of Harray are two large mounds, the more northerly of which contained two burial cists.

Places to visit:

17. Stones of Stenness, Mainland

Located on the SE shore of the Loch of Stenness on the E side of the B9055 and 600 m NW of its junction with the Kirkwall to Stromness road (A965). OS 1:50 000 map sheet 6; HY 306125.

The henge monument of the Stones of Stenness was probably constructed early in the third millennium BC and, impressive though the surviving standing stones are, the original appearance of the site must have been even more splendid. There were probably 12 standing stones surrounded by a deep rock-cut ditch and a substantial bank, with a single entrance-causeway facing towards the Barnhouse settlement (no. 3). The standing stones were set in holes up to about 1 m in depth and the holes were then filled with boulders to support the upright stones.

At the centre of the circle there is an almost square setting of stones, like an oversize domestic hearth, which contained tiny fragments of cremated bone, charcoal and sherds of Grooved Ware pottery, mixed with earth and small stones. Between the centre of the circle and the entrance two upright stones and a stone now lying flat are the remains of another setting.

above: Four of the great Stones of Stenness have survived the centuries

right: Was this the ritual focus of the circle ?

There are two outlying standing stones which may be associated with the Stones of Stenness and there were formerly two others; the Barnhouse Stone is situated 700 m to the SE and the Watch Stone 170 m to the NNW. The Watch Stone is a huge monolith, 5.6 m high.

Archaeology cannot answer the question 'What do these stones mean?', but the visitor walking between the Stones of Stenness and the Ring of

Brodgar, passing the Watch Stone and two further uprights to the SE of the farm of Brodgar, may have the impression of following a ceremonial way.

18. Ring of Brodgar, Mainland

Located between the lochs of Stenness and Harray on the W side of the B9055 and 1.5 km NW of the Stones of Stenness (no.14). OS 1:50 000 map sheet 6; HY 294133.

The Ring of Brodgar is the focus of the second major group of monuments in this area, which comprises imposing barrows, the Comet Stone and the henge monument with its stone circle. The deep ditch that surrounds the stone circle is broken by two opposing causeways; excavation has shown that the ditch was originally as much as 3 m deep and 9 m across, cut into solid rock, and there appears to have been no outer bank.

There were originally 60 stones in the circle, but only 36 stones remain in position, either as uprights or broken stumps. The stones are undecorated except for five Norse runes and a cross on a broken upright in the northern quadrant; the runes form a cryptogram giving a common name, *Bjorn.* The interior of the circle has not been excavated.

A trench was dug across the ditch in 1974

Scotland's climate worsened towards the end of the second millennium BC, becoming cooler and wetter. The great period of public building in Orkney was long over, and, apart from small burial mounds, the most numerous monuments of this period are burnt mounds. These are mounds of black soil and burnt stones, which are the debris from cooking in a particular way. Stones were heated on a hearth and dropped into tanks of water in order to boil joints of meat. Excavation can reveal the hearths and stone tanks along with the foundations of buildings; one such excavated site can be seen at Liddle, not far from the Isbister tomb (no.10).

From the middle of the first millennium BC, there was a trend in Orkney, as elsewhere, towards building large and substantial stone houses. This led to the era of broch-building, in the last few centuries BC, when fortified houses or brochs were constructed throughout northern Scotland and the western and northern islands. Although details of

Midhowe Broch overlooks Eynhallow Sound

their architecture may vary, in basic plan brochs are a uniform and highly impressive class of monument; they are circular dry-stone towers, from 11 m to 15 m in overall diameter at the base, and they were built with such thick walls (3.7 m to 4.6 m) that they could rise to considerable heights, although these are probably exceptional.

A single entrance at ground-level was the only opening in the smooth outer face of the broch, but inside there were openings into cells, stairways and galleries built within the thickness of the broch-wall. A ledge running horizontally round the inner face of most brochs at a height of 2 m or 3 m above the floor may have supported a timber gallery, and the roof, evidence for which does not survive, must also have been timber-framed.

Brochs were highly defensible structures in themselves but sometimes they were strengthened even further by encircling ramparts and ditches; such outlying defences are particularly well illustrated by the two brochs in State care, Gurness (no. 19) and Midhowe (no. 20). Three lines of rampart and ditch protect Gurness broch, while at Midhowe a single massive rampart was built, sandwiched between a pair of ditches. Burroughston broch (no. 21) is set within a wall, a ditch and an outer earthen rampart, and Burrian (no. 22) has four lines of defence. In some cases, it is possible that the earthwork defences represent an earlier fort to which a broch was added, rather than defences contemporary with the broch.

Defence was clearly a major factor in the design of brochs, but it is difficult to identify the underlying reason that made such defensive measures necessary. Society seems to have been turbulent and aggressive everywhere at this time but, in the absence of written sources, we cannot discover either by whom or against whom the brochs were built in any particular area. Brochs were permanently occupied family homes rather than occasional retreats; their internal fittings include hearths, storage tanks and often a water supply in the form of a natural spring, and a wide range of domestic equipment has been found in them. The basic economy of the families was still mixed farming and fishing.

The settlements that grew up around the brochs look very cluttered and crowded in the form in which they survive today, particularly at Gurness, but this is the result of several centuries of building and rebuilding and alterations to old houses. Whatever the social conditions that demanded the building of fortified towers, by the late second century AD conditions seem to have altered and brochs were gradually being modified, abandoned or even dismantled. This change in status is clearly seen at Gurness and Midhowe, where the broch-towers were used as sources of stone to build new structures both inside and outside the now abandoned brochs, and where the original outlying defences were slighted and built over.

It is possible that some at least of the Orcadian earth-houses belong to this period after the abandonment of brochs, but others may date to the last few centuries BC. The date and function of earth-houses are outstanding problems in the archaeology of the Orkneys and they will be solved only by excavation. They are most likely to have been underground storage cellars belonging to farmhouses.

Places to visit:

19. Broch of Gurness, Mainland

Located about 28 km NW of Kirkwall on the A965 and A966; carpark; Visitor Centre; guidebook. OS 1:50 000 map sheet 6; HY 381268.

Like most brochs in the Northern Isles, Gurness was built with a thick stone base to the tower, which made it possible for the walls to rise to a considerable height. The surviving masonry is incomplete, owing to collapse and stone-robbing, but the tower might well have risen originally to a height of some 12 m or more. The broch was encircled by three lines of ditch and rampart with an entrance causeway at the E, though much of these early defences and buildings has been destroyed by coastal erosion. The precise date at which the broch was built is unknown but by

analogy with brochs elsewhere it is likely to have been in the first century BC. By the third century AD the broch-tower had lost its original defensive character and had been converted into a domestic dwelling.

There seems initially to have been a row of semi-detached houses partially encircling the broch-tower. These were essentially sub-rectangular buildings with good dry-stone walls and carefully kerbed hearths, but they were divided into rooms and alcoves by upright slabs and minor walls which proliferated over the years.

In front of the Visitor Centre are the foundations of houses that had been built on top of the ruins of the broch-village (removed during excavation and rebuilt here). One is a five-celled house which was built in Pictish times, probably in the sixth or seventh century AD. In the Visitor Centre may be seen a stone carved with typical Pictish symbols.

above: Aerial view of the Broch of Gurness
left: Inside the broch with its hearth, well and partitions

There was Norse activity on the site in the ninth century, for the grave of a well-to-do woman was discovered in the upper core of the inner rampart on the N or seaward side of the entrance-causeway. She had been buried in a roughly constructed stone-lined pit, and some of her personal belongings had been placed in the grave with her. At her breast there were two large oval brooches made of bronze; on the corroded back of one of these brooches were discovered traces of fabric which showed that the body had been dressed in finely woven wool. An iron necklet hung round her neck, a small iron sickle lay at her right side and knife with a wooden handle at her left (these finds are in Tankerness House Museum).

20. Broch of Midhowe, Rousay

Located on the W coast of the island about 8 km from Trumland pier; signposted path; guidebook. OS 1:50 000 map sheet 6; HY 371306. On the Westness Walk.

The shores of Eynhallow Sound abound with the remains of brochs, both along the coast of the mainland and along the Rousay shore, and they must have been a daunting sight in their original condition. The Broch of Midhowe stands in a particularly fine situation on a very rocky shore with a narrow creek or geo on either side, so that it occupies in effect a promontory. The landward side is barred by a formidable triple line of defence, consisting of two ditches with a massive stone rampart set between them. The broch itself survives to a height of 4.3 m, with a ledge on the inner face of the wall which carried a first-floor gallery.

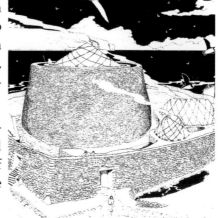

The broch wall has an internal gallery at ground-level, an unusual feature among the normally solid based brochs of the Northern Isles, and the effect of this hollow base was to weaken the broch; at some

Midhowe in its heyday, reconstructed by AR Braby

Midhowe Broch is crowded with hearths, cisterns, alcoves and screens

stage in its occupation the ground gallery had to be blocked partially when the wall threatened to collapse. The wall was also buttressed on the outside by stone slabs set on end and side by side. The broch is almost circular, with an overall diameter of about 18 m and an internal diameter of about 9.6 m.

The doorway into the broch is well-preserved and impressive, with checks for doors at the inner end of the passage and at a distance of about 2.3 m from the outer end. Between the two lie openings into cells built within the thickness of the wall. The cell on the right of the entrance has an excellent corbelled roof, while the left-hand cell opens into the gallery which runs round inside the broch wall almost to the back of the other cell. There was originally an upper mural gallery as well, to which access was gained by a stairway opening from inside the broch.

The inside of the broch is full of slab-partitions, alcoves, hearths and tanks, most of which represent secondary rather than original building activities. A stone-kerbed hearth slightly to the right of centre on entering possesses a carefully constructed stone socket on either side which would probably have held the uprights for a spit across the fire. Beside and slightly overlapped by the hearth there is a fine stone tank with a well-fitting slab lid; this was a water-tank supplied by good spring water which still flows up through a crack in the rock. Against the broch wall to the left on entering there is the product of a remarkable feat of dry-stone building: an alcove has been formed by a large slab, almost 2.3 m tall, set on end and supporting a pier of dry-stone masonry, which soars up and becomes a corbelled roof over the alcove.

There was once an extensive complex of buildings partially surrounding the broch-tower but this has suffered from coastal erosion.

Many artefacts were found during the excavation of Midhowe, mostly domestic equipment but with a few surprises. Among the latter were fragments of a bronze patera or ladle and some sherds of pottery, all of which have a Roman origin and must have reached Midhowe as a

The grand entrance into Midhowe broch

47

result of raiding or trading expeditions. Lumps of iron slag and the remains of a smelting hearth in one of the secondary buildings to the N of the broch-tower demonstrate that iron-working was carried out on the site, although no iron artefacts have survived. Bronze-working was also a local activity, for fragments of crucibles and moulds used in casting bronze objects were found. Three ring-headed pins and three penannular brooches made of bronze indicate the type of fastenings that were used in personal dress, and a number of stone and bone spindle whorls shows that some garments at least were woven, perhaps using long-handled combs made of whalebone to beat down the threads on the loom. Most of the objects recovered were made either of bone or stone and they represent a wide range of everyday tools from bone awls to whetstones and querns.

21. Burroughston, Shapinsay (Orkney Islands Council)

Located 150 m ENE of Easthouse near the NE tip of the island. OS 1:50 000 map sheet 5; HY 540210.

The broch known as Hillock of Burroughston stands close to a rocky shore. The lower part of its wall is intact, and the entrance passage has checks and a bar-hole to secure a door. There is a guard-cell to one side of the passage, and another cell within the broch-wall in the SW arc. This was a well-defended broch, for there are outer works, in the form of a wall, a deep ditch and a rampart, which are likely once to have encircled it entirely. Later building outside the broch destroyed the outer defences on the seaward side.

22. Broch of Burrian, North Ronaldsay (OIC access agreement)

Located at the S tip of the island; access along foreshore. OS 1:50 000 map sheet 5; HY 762513.

Set on a rocky promontory, Burrian is an excellent example of a broch with outer defences, here consisting of four lines of ramparts guarding the landward side of the broch. Despite coastal erosion, the broch is still very impressive, and there are traces of domestic buildings outside it. Excavation in the 1870s revealed evidence of settlement here in Pictish times, long after the broch had outlived its original purpose.

23. Grain, Mainland

Located 800 m NW of Kirkwall harbour (A965). OS 1:50 000 map sheet 6; HY 441116.

This is a particularly fine earth-house, with the unusual feature of a flight of steps leading from ground level down into the end of the passage. The upper part of the stair was rebuilt when the site was taken into State care but the lower part is original. The passage runs in a pronounced curve until it opens out into a bean-shaped chamber, and both have roofs of flat slabs. In the chamber the slabs are supported at a height of about 1.5 m by four free-standing stone piers. Both chamber and passage are carefully built of dry-stone masonry, and they were

quite empty when first explored. A second earth-house and remains of ground-level buildings were found nearby in 1982, and it seems likely that both earth-houses were once part of a single domestic settlement.

24. Rennibister, Mainland

Located 6.5 km WNW of Kirkwall (A965) in a working farmyard. OS 1:50 000 map sheet 6; HY 397125.

On 12 November 1926 part of the farmyard at Rennibister collapsed beneath the weight of a threshing machine, exposing a remarkable underground chamber. The walls are constructed in dry-stone masonry which curves inwards to form a corbelled roof over the oval chamber. Extra support for the roof (and the earth above it) is provided by four stone pillars, and five small recesses, rather like open cupboards, have been built into the walls.

Original access to the chamber was down a gently sloping passage, with a rough step at the chamber entrance to break the drop down to the floor of the chamber. The passage is low and narrow; to get down to the chamber it would have been necessary to crawl.

When it was discovered, the chamber contained a mass of human bones. The bones represented six adults and about 12 children of various ages and their presence in the earth-house is a mystery. Rennibister is the only Orcadian earth-house to have yielded burials of any sort, and it is most unlikely that it was originally designed as a burial-vault.

The earth-house would originally have been entered from a roundhouse built of stone and timber
(reconstruction AR Braby)

By the fourth century AD, the name *Picti* had begun to appear in the works of classical authors concerned with northern Britain, and it is certain that, by the sixth century, Orkney was part of the Pictish kingdom. Adomnan, the biographer of St Columba, records that there were Orcadians at the court of the Pictish king, Bridei, during Columba's visit around AD 565; the Orcadians are described as hostages in a way that suggests that, although they had their own local ruler, they recognised Bridei as their overlord. Pictish Orcadians were the descendants of the broch-builders, and their farmsteads are often the latest buildings on the sites of abandoned brochs, as at Gurness (no.19).

The most distinctively Pictish objects found in Orkney are the decorated stone slabs known as Pictish symbol stones. None survives as a standing monument, but a cast of the slab found in the Early Christian cemetery on the Brough of Birsay has been erected on the site and gives a good impression of the original appearance of such stones. There is a fine collection of stones in Tankerness House Museum and a small example in the Visitor Centre at Gurness (no.19). The repertoire of Pictish art included abstract symbols, fantasy animals and realistic designs of animals and human figures, and the standard of craftsmanship was often very high. The purpose of the symbol stones is obscure; about 250 stones have been found, distributed over the whole of Pictland from Shetland to the Firth of Forth and dating from the centuries between about AD 500 and 900, and some variety of function would not be surprising. Among the explanations that have been put forward in recent years are that they were tombstones, personal memorial monuments, landmarkers showing territorial boundaries, or public monuments commemorating important marriage alliances between great families.

Orkney's first contact with Christianity is likely to have been in the sixth century, but conversion is thought to have been gradual and

Bone pins were used by the Picts as the models to make clay moulds for casting bronze pins (all found on the Brough of Birsay)

Seal's tooth with runes inscribed on it, from the Brough of Birsay

it may not have been until the eighth century that the islands could be counted as fully within the authority of the Church. The upstanding early churches that survive cannot be dated before about 1100.

The Brough of Birsay is a site of exceptional interest and importance, for its known settlement spanned not just the Pictish period but the Norse period as well and continued into medieval times.

Orkney was first settled by Norsemen around AD 800 and they soon became a nodal point on the western seaways. The Norse earldom of the Orkneys, Shetland and Caithness grew into a powerful political unit, and the events recorded in *Orkneyinga Saga* make exciting reading. Much of the early part of the *Saga* is fictitious, but there is a strong element of reliable history in the later chapters. The *Saga* ends with the terrible burning of Bishop Adam at Halkirk in Caithness, a deed which led to the murder of Earl John in the cellar of a Thurso inn in 1231 and thereby ended the Norse line of earls.

Although the incoming Norsemen adopted many ideas and traditions from the indigenous Picts, once the Norse settlement was firmly established, the Pictish element lost its separate identity and the cultural life of Orkney became entirely that of a Norse earldom. The far-ranging interests and activities of Viking-Age Orcadians are well attested by the surviving monuments of the late eleventh and twelfth centuries – by the round church at Orphir with its links with Jerusalem and the Crusades, and, above all, by the superb Cathedral of St Magnus in Kirkwall, founded by Earl Rognvald in 1137.

W Douglas Simpson has vividly evoked the impact on the small community that was then Kirkwall of the building of the cathedral. 'Let us picture in our minds the concourse of highly skilled imported craftsmen who must have settled down among the dry-stone and turf-roofed huts of the local inhabitants. There would be the skilled masons and imagers, the carpenters and plasters, the glaziers and the tilers and the painters, the workers in metal, the jewellers and enamellers and the makers or merchants of rich and costly vestments and altar-cloths. The advent of all these craftsmen-artists, and of the swarm of purveyors who supplied their needs, must have involved a social revolution in twelfth-century Kirkwall. And into the midst of this hive of creative, artistic activity comes the great building Bishop himself with his court – the ordainer and deviser, under his noble patron, of the whole vast enterprise, transferring to the immediate neighbourhood of the rising cathedral his own Episcopal residence from the outlying station of Birsay.'

The bishop in question was William the Old (1102–68), and it has been suggested that the earliest part of the Bishop's Palace was his Episcopal residence.

Places to visit:

25. Brough of Birsay, Mainland

Located at the NW point of Mainland, 32 km NW of Kirkwall (A965, A986, A966); signposted causeway to tidal island; guidebook. Crossing is impossible during the period approximately three hours before High Water to three hours after. High Water is one hour before High Water Kirkwall, which is posted at the Harbourmaster's office there. OS 1:50 000 map sheet 6; HY 239285.

The island is only about 21 hectares in extent, rising to high steep cliffs on the W, where puffins live, and sloping gently towards the shore on the E, where there are the remains of an extensive and interesting settlement of Pictish and Norse times.

top: Aerial view of Brough of Birsay
above: Foundations of a Norse house

Only a small well is visible of what was once an extensive Pictish settlement, but excavation has shown that, beneath the later buildings, there are traces of oval houses of the seventh and eighth centuries. In the later churchyard stands a cast of the superb Pictish symbol stone which was discovered here, shattered into fragments; carved on it are three bearded warriors, armed with square shields and spears, an eagle, a fantasy beast sometimes known as the 'swimming elephant' and the symbols known as the crescent and V-rod and the mirror case.

Most of the visible remains belong to the Viking Age or later, although again the original extent of the settlement was much larger. On the slope beyond the churchyard are some of the finest examples of Norse hall-houses ever found in Scotland. These are typical family houses of the ninth and tenth centuries and consist essentially of a single long hall, furnished with benches on either side of a hearth, and built of stone and turf. Part of a very large example of such a building may be seen close to the edge of the cliff.

The complicated mass of walls between the churchyard and the cliff represents a series of successive houses built between the ninth and twelfth centuries. The church itself was built in the early twelfth century, and it was served by an ecclesiastical community living in the buildings round a courtyard on its N side. Although small, this was a beautiful Romanesque church of quite sophisticated design. There are altar-niches on either side of the entrance from the nave into the square chancel, and a semi-circular apse beyond the chancel; traces of walling outside the W door of the nave suggest that there may once have been a porch or tower.

Excavation has yielded many fine objects of Pictish, Norse and medieval date, some of which are in Tankerness House Museum.

26. Brough of Deerness, Mainland (Orkney Islands Council)

Located about 30 km ESE of Kirkwall on the A960 and B9050 to Skaill, thence a minor road northwards to a carpark; signposted path. Great care should be taken on the cliff path. OS 1:50 000 map sheet 6; HY 596087.

A most dramatic spot was chosen for this settlement – a high promontory detached from the mainland except at shore-level and surrounded by near-vertical cliffs. The rampart across its landward end seems almost superfluous given its natural defences. In the grass on the flat top of the promontory can be made out the foundations of many oblong buildings, and among them is a small stone chapel in a walled enclosure. The houses have not been excavated but the chapel

Remote and secure: the Brough of Deerness

proved to have replaced an earlier timber and stone version and both are likely to be Norse in date.

The many pits are the result of target-practice during World War II.

27. Cubbie Roo's Castle, Wyre

Located 1.2 km SW of the landing place on the NW side of the island. OS 1:50 000 map sheet 6; HY 441263.

Standing on the crest of a small ridge are the remains of a rare Norse castle. *Orkneyinga Saga* records that, in the mid twelfth century, Wyre was the home of an outstanding Norwegian named Kolbein Hruga, who built a fine stone castle as a safe stronghold for himself and his family. His name has become corrupted as Cubbie Roo, *Kubbie* being a Norse nickname for *Kolbein*. The fact that the castle stands close both to a twelfth-century church and to a modern farm, whose name, the Bu of Wyre, reflects the great Norse hall which preceded it, demonstrates that this was indeed the site of the family seat.

The original building was a small stone tower set within encircling ramparts, the entire fortified area being only 23 m by 29 m in extent. The outer defences consisted of a ditch, almost 2 m deep to its flat bottom, with a low earthen rampart outside it and a strong

stone wall on its inner side. The S part of these defences has not survived for it was demolished to make room for later buildings at a time when the castle had lost its defensive character. Inside the wall a second shallow ditch was dug into the natural bedrock in order to leave a central platform on which the tower was built. The entrance through all these outer defences is on the E, where the outer ditch was bridged by flat stone slabs resting on piers.

A reconstruction of the Norse castle under attack

The tower itself is almost 8 m square, with thick walls surviving to a height of about 2 m; only the ground floor of the tower remains, and the narrow ledge which supported the joists for the first floor can be seen on the inner face of the N wall. The ground floor was probably used as a storeroom, accessible only by ladder from the first floor, and the entrance into the tower must have been in the first floor above. A roughly rectangular tank has been dug into the rock floor of the storeroom, possibly to hold an emergency water supply. Two narrow slits open through the W and S walls, each rebated near the outer end to take a wooden window-frame. The outside of the tower was originally plastered. It is impossible to be certain how high the tower stood when first built; at least three floors would have been necessary in order to achieve a reasonably clear view over Gairsay Sound.

Wings were later added to the tower, and domestic buildings eventually filled the space around it and even extended over the levelled earlier defences.

28. St Mary's Church, Wyre

Located 1.2 km S of the landing place on the NW side of the island. OS 1:50 000 map sheet 6; HY 443262.

This small chapel was built in the late twelfth century and partially restored in the late nineteenth or early twentieth century. It has a rectangular nave and a square-ended chancel, with an arch between the two, and two lintelled windows survive. Traces of the original plaster can be seen both in the nave and in the chancel, and the present harling on the outside seems to have replaced plasterwork.

29. Orphir Church, Mainland

Located about 14.5 km SW of Kirkwall (A964) on the shore of Scapa Flow. OS 1:50 000 map sheet 6; HY 334044.

The remains of Scotland's only surviving circular medieval church may be seen at Orphir on the mainland of Orkney overlooking Scapa Flow. About two-thirds of the church was dismantled to provide stone for the later parish church which, until itself demolished, partially overlaid it; the line of the nave wall may be seen and the apse is still intact. Light was provided by a round-arched window in the E end of the apse, and beneath the window is a seating for an altar. The nave would also have had a vaulted ceiling with a central skylight.

The church was built in the first half of the twelfth century and was dedicated to St Nicholas. Its circular plan was derived ultimately from the Church of the Holy Sepulchre in Jerusalem; this was the period of the great Crusades, and the circular church became popular over much of Europe as the returning Crusaders brought with them the idea of copying the famous church in Jerusalem. Earl Haakon Paulsson, who died in 1122, went

on pilgrimage to Jerusalem and his seat in Orkney was at Orphir. He may well have instigated the building of what *Orkneyinga Saga* describes as a 'magnificent church'.

The same passage in the *Saga* describes the main hall of the earl's residence, or Bu, which stood beside the church. The remains of a large building have

Was this Earl Haakon's 'magnificent church'?

been excavated and are still visible near the round church but they cannot be dated with certainty to the same period.

Beside one of the modern farm buildings, close to the road, are the underhouse, tail-race and lade of a horizontal water-mill; this was part of the earlier Norse farm and is the earliest evidence in the Northern Isles for the type of mill that later became very common.

A Visitor Centre in the carpark provides information on Norse sites mentioned in *Orkneyinga Saga* and on the history of archaeological excavation at the Earl's Bu (Orkney Islands Council).

30. St Magnus Church, Egilsay

Located about 700 m NE of the pier on the W side of the island. OS 1:50 000 map sheet 6; HY 466303.

This small and low-lying island is dominated by the beautiful church of St Magnus. It consists of the normal rectangular nave and square-ended chancel but it has the addition of a tall round tower at the W end. It belongs to a group of churches built in the twelfth century on both sides of the North Sea.

The tower has survived to a height of 14.9 m but it is thought to have been some 4.5 m higher originally and to have had four or five storeys; the ground floor has a window facing S, the first floor has one facing W, the second floor E and the third floor has four windows, one to each quarter of the

St Magnus Church with its round tower

compass. The base of the tower is 3 m in diameter internally, narrowing to 2 m towards the top. The entire building is now roofless, but an early nineteenth-century sketch shows a gabled roof of stone slabs over nave and chancel and a conical slab roof on the tower. The gables were finished with crow-steps.

The church is dedicated to St Magnus, who was murdered on the island around AD 1117 at the order of the rival Earl Haakon so that the latter might rule alone over Orkney.

31. Eynhallow Church, Eynhallow

Located on the S side of the island. OS 1:50 000 map sheet 6; HY 359288.

Eynhallow is a small uninhabited island lying between Rousay and the E coast of mainland Orkney, a quiet haven for birds and seals. Its name comes from the Norse *Eyin-Helga* or Holy Isle and indicates its early importance as an ecclesiastical site. The island would appear to have had a monastic settlement in the twelfth century; *Orkneyinga Saga* relates how the foster-son of the great Kolbein Hruga of Wyre was kidnapped from Eynhallow in 1155, and it is most probable that the boy had been sent there to be educated by the monks. The only surviving building which is as early as the twelfth century is the church, which was reconstructed as a dwelling house in the sixteenth century.

The church consisted of a rectangular nave with a porch at its W end and a square-ended chancel at the E end. Of the walling visible today, only the porch, the W and E gables of the nave and the lower part of the inner face of the chancel walls are original. The rest represents the sixteenth-century reconstruction.

32. Pierowall Church, Westray

Located in Pierowall village. OS 1:50 000 map sheet 5; HY 439488.

The Bay of Pierowall on the E coast of Westray has long been a focus of settlement. A large cemetery of pagan Viking-Age graves was discovered in the sand dunes here in the nineteenth century, and it was to this safe natural harbour that Earl Rognvald and his men came in 1136 at the start of his subjugation of Orkney.

The oldest fabric of the surviving church dates from the thirteenth century, but most of the visible building represents alterations carried out in the seventeenth century – the date 1674 is carved on the S skewput of the gable separating nave from chancel. The original church consisted of a rectangular nave and chancel, but the nave was widened in the seventeenth century and the chancel was reconstructed as a 'laird's aisle', which is out of alignment with the nave by being canted southwards. Two grave-slabs have been built into the wall at the E end of the church; they are good examples of seventeenth-century funerary monuments.

33. Westside Church, Westray

Located on the S shore of the island, 5.7 km S of Pierowall. OS 1:50 000 map sheet 5; HY 455431.

This church almost certainly owes its location to the presence nearby of an important settlement of late Norse date, which has been identified by excavation about 70 m to the W. The twelfth-century church consisted of a rectangular nave and a barrel-vaulted chancel, but an extension was added at the W end of the nave at some later period.

34. St Boniface Church, Papa Westray (Orkney Islands Council)

Located on the W coast of the island, approached by a track from the road between Holland and North Hill. OS 50 000 map sheet 5; HY 488527.

Built in the twelfth century, this church originally had both nave and chancel, but the latter was demolished and the space was later used for the burial enclosure of the Traills of

Holland. The nave was extended westwards in 1700 to accommodate an internal gallery served by an external stair. The church has recently been refurbished.

In the graveyard is a fine example of a twelfth-century hogback tombstone; made from a block of red sandstone, it is carved with a deep groove along its ridge and three rows of 'roof-tiles' along either side. It lies E–W and is accompanied by a small headstone.

On the seaward side of the churchyard there is an extensive prehistoric settlement, severely eroded by the sea and partially excavated.

35. St Magnus Cathedral, Kirkwall, Mainland (Orkney Islands Council)

Located in Broad Street, Kirkwall; guidebook. OS 1:50 000 sheet 6; HY 449108.

Work on this superb cathedral began in 1137 and the choir was ready for worship within about 15 years, although the entire building was not finished until more than 300 years later. The west front with its three decorated doorways was built in the thirteenth century, making use of red and white sandstone to striking effect.

Kirkwall's market cross of 1621 is now housed in the north transept of the cathedral.

Kirkwall's Cathedral of St Magnus

36. Bishop's Palace, Kirkwall, Mainland

Located in Kirkwall, S of the Cathedral; guidebook. OS 1:50 000 map sheet 6; HY 449108.

The main rectangular block of the Bishop's Palace forms what is known as a hall-house, comprising a series of cellars, above which the major apartment or hall was built. Only the lowest portion survives of this early building in which the Norwegian King Haakon died in 1263 after defeat at the Battle of Largs, but, like his own great hall in Bergen, it would have been a sombrely splendid residence.

In the second period of building, Bishop Reid (1541-58) reconstructed and heightened the main block and built the round tower at the NW angle. The tower has five storeys and an attic and is furnished with gun-loops. An arched niche above the modern street contains a statue thought to be of St Olaf. There is an excellent view of St Magnus Cathedral from the top of the tower, and an information board explains the sequence of building the cathedral.

There were originally other buildings alongside, including a chapel and two large square towers. One of the towers, called the Manse Tower, was probably the Bishop's manse or private residence.

The Scottish earldom, 1469–1615

After the murder of the last of the Norse Earls of Orkney in 1231, the title passed to the son of the Earl of Angus, a Scot who in respect of his title owed allegiance to the Norwegian Crown. Following the Battle of Largs in 1263 and the loss of the Western Isles to the Scottish Crown as a result of the Treaty of Perth in 1266, only the Northern Isles remained Norse possessions. The increasing control of Orkney by earls who were of Scottish origin, culminating in the appointment of Henry Sinclair, Earl of Roslin, to the earldom in 1379, led to changes in the ownership of land and the break-up of Norse systems of tenure.

The Northern Isles were officially held by the Sinclairs of the Norwegian and later of the Danish Crown until their annexation to the Scottish Crown as a result of the dowry agreement made on the marriage of James III of Scotland with Margaret, the daughter of King Christian I of Norway and Denmark, in 1468. By this agreement Orkney was held as a pledge, redeemable by the payment of 50 000 Rhenish florins, but the following year it remained unpaid and Shetland was therefore pledged for 8000 florins. Two years later, as the pledges had not been redeemed, the earldom of Orkney and lordship of Shetland were annexed to the Scottish Crown. In the following century Norse systems of land-holding and government steadily gave way to Scottish customs, and indeed Scottish landowners, and by the late seventeenth century the Norse language was spoken by the inhabitants of only two or three parishes.

In 1564 Mary Queen of Scots made a grant of the royal estates in Orkney and Shetland to Robert Stewart, her half-brother, and a natural son of James V. His tenure of office has been concisely narrated: 'This miscreant, having secured in addition the whole temporal estates of the bishopric by an excambion (exchange) effected in 1568, and having become Earl of Orkney in 1581, spent the rest of his life – with the exception of a short period during which he was imprisoned, partly as a penalty for improper negotiations with Denmark – in oppressing the islanders for his own personal advantage'.

The architectural legacy of Earl Robert and his son, Patrick (1592–1615) is, however, of outstanding interest. The palace at Birsay, begun for Earl Robert in 1574, is an impressive courtyard building, the interior of which was formerly richly decorated. Earl Patrick was even more ambitious and his palace at Kirkwall, begun in 1606, is spacious and well-proportioned. In contrast, Noltland Castle on the island of Westray is a grim military building dating to between 1560 and 1571; the lavish provision of gun-loops betrays the ruthlessness of Gilbert Balfour for whom it was built.

Many of grand houses of the seventeenth and eighteenth centuries had dovecotes in their grounds to provide meat and eggs for the table. The circular dovecote at Rendall is a unique survival in Orkney of this early type of dovecote.

Places to visit:

37. Earl's Palace, Kirkwall, Mainland

Located in Kirkwall, S of the Cathedral; guidebook. OS 1:50 000 map sheet 6; HY 449107.

'The Earl's Palace forms three sides of an oblong square, and has, even in its ruins, the air of an elegant yet massive structure, uniting, as was usual in the residence of feudal princes, the character of a palace and of a castle.'

Thus Sir Walter Scott in his novel, *The Pirate* , describes both the architectural interest of the Earl's Palace and its atmosphere.

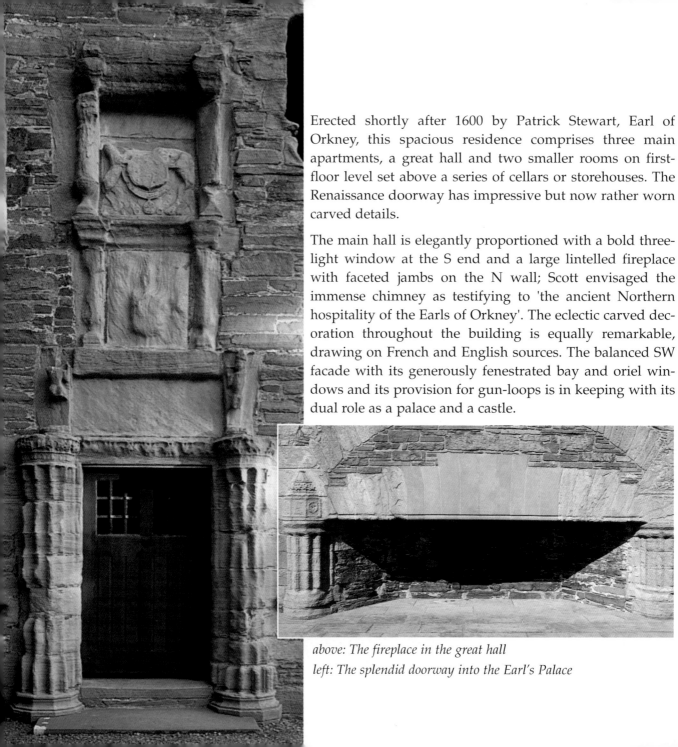

Erected shortly after 1600 by Patrick Stewart, Earl of Orkney, this spacious residence comprises three main apartments, a great hall and two smaller rooms on first-floor level set above a series of cellars or storehouses. The Renaissance doorway has impressive but now rather worn carved details.

The main hall is elegantly proportioned with a bold three-light window at the S end and a large lintelled fireplace with faceted jambs on the N wall; Scott envisaged the immense chimney as testifying to 'the ancient Northern hospitality of the Earls of Orkney'. The eclectic carved decoration throughout the building is equally remarkable, drawing on French and English sources. The balanced SW facade with its generously fenestrated bay and oriel windows and its provision for gun-loops is in keeping with its dual role as a palace and a castle.

above: The fireplace in the great hall
left: The splendid doorway into the Earl's Palace

38. Tankerness House Museum, Kirkwall, Mainland (Orkney Islands Council)

Located in Broad Street, Kirkwall. OS 1:50 000 map sheet 6; HY 448108. Now a museum.

A particularly fine example of an early town house, Tankerness House was built in the sixteenth century as the archdeanery for St Magnus Cathedral. One of the archdeacons who lived here is commemorated on the armorial panel over the entrance gateway – M G F for Master Gilbert Fulzie and the date 1574. The gateway and the north wing are the oldest surviving parts of the house, which was extensively rebuilt in the eighteenth century. It was restored in 1968 as a museum, with displays tracing the story of Orkney's past from prehistoric times. There is a charming courtyard and at the back of the house a large and peaceful garden full of summer colour.

A replica of the mercat cross stands in front of the Cathedral, and across Broad Street can be seen the archway into Tankerness House

39. Earl's Palace, Birsay, Mainland

Located near the shore in the village and at the end of the public road, some 32 km from Kirkwall (A965, A986, A966). OS 1:50 000 map sheet 6; HY 248277.

Overlooking Birsay Bay are the austere remains of the residence of the late-sixteenth-century Earls of Orkney. The palace was constructed around a courtyard with projecting rectangular towers at three corners. The range on the N is rather later than the main period of building. The corner towers, the courtyard and the N range are provided with numerous gun-loops. Drawings made in the seventeenth and eighteenth centuries give an impression of the palace in its original more open setting with gardens and plots to the E;

they also show the elegant S facade with its central doorway and the initials of Robert, Earl of Orkney, above the lintel, and the date of 1574 over a window above it. There were also decorated pediments above the windows.

The palace was described in 1633 as a 'sumptuous and stately building'. The reception rooms on the upper floor were richly decorated, and the ceilings were painted with biblical subjects and texts, such as the Flood and the Entry into Jerusalem.

40. Noltland Castle, Westray

Located 800 m W of Pierowall; guide-leaflet. OS 1:50 000 map sheet 5; HY 429486.

Noltland Castle is an austere and formidable stronghold. Begun in 1560, it is an excellent example of a Z-plan castle, with towers at diagonally opposite corners of a main block; this allowed for increased accommodation and possibly greater privacy than did the simple tower-house, but it also had important defensive advantages for the use of firearms. At Noltland, the almost extravagant provision of gun-loops provides a telling character assessment of the builder, Gilbert Balfour.

The approach to the doorway is through a courtyard of later date than the castle and the entrance in the SW tower is well-covered by gun-loops. The kitchen and storerooms were on the ground floor, and an unusually spacious stairway led from the entrance up to the great hall on the first floor. Do not miss the richly carved capital at the top of the stair or the extensive view from the eastern battlements.

41. Rendall Dovecote, Mainland (Orkney Islands Council)

Located some 11 km N of Finstown on a minor road off the A966. OS 1:50 000 map sheet 6; HY 422207.

This restored dovecote was built in the seventeenth century to serve the family living in the Hall of Rendall. It is circular with a tapering profile and four protruding string-courses which were designed to foil the attempts of rats to climb the wall; inside, the nesting-boxes for the pigeons are formed simply by gaps left in the rough wall-face. The birds entered through the roof.

Nineteenth- and twentieth-century monuments

Click Mill, Dounby, is an attractive example of a horizontal water-mill, a type once common in Orkney and particularly in Shetland in recent centuries (and now known from Norse times at Orphir, no. 29). Tormiston Mill is a classic nineteenth-century mill with a large vertical water-wheel, such as can still be seen elsewhere in Orkney. The two farm museums at Corrigall and Kirbuster present a fascinating insight into rural life in the eighteenth and nineteenth centuries.

The impressive martello towers in Hoy are testimony not to the defence of Orkney against Napoleonic invaders, as is so often assumed, but against the navy and privateers of the United States of America. The United States declared war on Britain in June 1812 as a result of British harassment of American vessels trading with Napoleon's allies; American successes in western and northern waters and particularly in threatening the Baltic trade made the assembly place for convoys especially vulnerable. Vessels met in the Sound of Longhope and then, under the protection of a warship, crossed the North Sea. Artillery defence of the anchorage was

Inside the Click Mill at Dounby

provided between 1813 and 1815 by the construction of a battery and tower at Hackness on the south side and by a tower at Crockness on the north.

There are many reminders of World Wars I and II in Orkney – batteries, airfields, block-ships, the Churchill Barriers – but the most moving is undoubtedly the Italian Chapel on Lamb Holm, in the care of Orkney Islands Council. Scapa Flow was a vital naval base and there are huge red-painted sheds dating from 1917–18, including an oil-pumping station at Lyness, and to the south, the facade of a remarkable 1940s art deco theatre, originally built for servicemen and women but later converted into a private house.

Places to visit:

42. Click Mill, Dounby, Mainland

Located 3.5 km NE of Dounby (B9057). OS 1:50 000 map sheet 6; HY 325228.

Horizontal water-mills were never as numerous in Orkney as they were in Shetland, where natural water-power is far greater, but a fine example has been preserved in working order near Dounby. It is known as a click mill or clack mill from the sound that the machinery makes when running. The charac-teristic feature of these mills is that the wood-en water-wheel is set horizontally instead of vertically. It is thought that this type of mill may have been introduced into Scotland from Ireland where examples have been dated to the mid first millennium AD. This particular mill was built in the early nineteenth century but it follows the same pattern as earlier mills.

The water ran past the horizontal wheel and powered the millstones above

43. Boardhouse Mill, Mainland (Orkney Islands Council)

Located beside the A967 Stromness to Birsay road, about 1.5 km SE of Birsay village; carpark. OS 1:50 000 map sheet 6; HY 254274.

The younger of the two Barony Corn Mills at Boardhouse, this imposing mill was completed in 1873. There are three pairs of huge millstones, driven by an iron water-wheel more than 4 m in diameter.

Traditionally the mill ground the bere barley grown in the fertile Birsay fields and, restored to working order, it is the only mill still producing beremeal for bannocks.

44. Tormiston Mill, Mainland

Located about 15 km WNW of Kirkwall (A965); carpark; Visitor Centre. OS 1:50 000 map sheet 6; HY 319125.

This three-storey corn-mill has been skilfully restored, and its great iron water-wheel is intact, the water carried along an unusual stone-built aqueduct. The ground floor holds a display about Orkney's ancient monuments, the first floor a craft shop and the second floor a restaurant; some of the mill's internal machinery has been preserved, including the millstones.

45. Corrigall, Mainland (Orkney Islands Council)

Located about 9 km NW of Finstown on a minor road off the A986; carpark; leaflet. OS 1:50 000 map sheet 6; HY 324193.

Restored and furnished as a museum of farming life, this extensive homestead dates from the mid eighteenth century and includes a dwelling house, a byre and a barn with stables at one end and a corn-drying kiln at the other. The dwelling was originally a longhouse with a byre at one end.

46. Kirbuster, Mainland (Orkney Islands Council)

Located about 4.5 km N of Dounby on a minor road off the A986; carpark; leaflet. OS 1:50 000 map sheet 6; HY 282254.

This attractive homestead with its sheltered garden has been restored as a farm and folk museum. The house was built in 1723 and is more spacious than the average. It retains interesting early features such as a bed alcove (a neuk-bed) set into the wall and an open hearth, the smoke from which found its way out through a central smoke stack. The outbuildings include a pigsty, a smithy and a barn with a circular corn-drying kiln.

47. Martello Tower, Hackness, Hoy

Located on the NE tip of the peninsula of South Walls.
OS 1:50 000 map sheet 7; ND 338912.

The function of the tower was to provide a firm foundation for a 24-pounder cannon and living quarters for the non-commissioned officer (NCO) and gunners. The ground plan of the tower is elliptical, for the seaward wall is twice as thick as that facing inland to provide additional protection against bombardment. Inside the upper floors are circular with the cannon carriage on the open upper storey. The barrack room on the first floor housed the gunners, with a separate cubicle for the NCO. The only door into the tower is at a height of about 4 m above ground level outside, reached by a ladder and leading into the barrack room. The ground floor contains various stores

and the all-important magazine; the stairs leading to these floors are situated within the thickness of the seaward wall. The towers were refurbished in 1866 and were used in World War I.

Beyond the tower to the NW is a battery for eight 24-pounder guns, set behind a stone parapet. It was backed up by barracks for the gunners, storerooms and a magazine for the ammunition.

48. Pumping Station and Scapa Flow Visitor Centre, Lyness, Hoy (Orkney Islands Council)

Located on the E coast of Hoy on the B9047, carpark. OS 1:50 000 map sheet 7; ND 309946.

Built in 1917 to service the Royal Navy in World War I, steam-powered pumps brought oil from tankers at the piers into four 12 000-ton storage tanks. The fuel for the pumps was originally coal, but they were converted to oil in 1936, when 12 more tanks were built (one of which survives). The Station also acts now as an interpretation centre for wartime Scapa Flow and the Lyness naval base.

A good example of a pillbox can be seen beside the naval cemetery at Lyness.

above: Martello tower at Hackness
below: Lyness naval base

49. Churchill Barriers and Italian Chapel, Lamb Holm (Orkney Islands Council)

Located 12 km S of Kirkwall on the A961, carpark. OS 1:50 000 map sheets 6,7, Barriers HY 483012–ND 476948, Chapel HY 488006.

Lamb Holm is linked to mainland Orkney by the first of the Churchill Barriers that were built during World War II to restrict access into Scapa Flow. Another three barriers span the sounds between Lamb Holm and Glimps Holm, Glimps Holm and Burray, and Burray and South Ronaldsay. They were built with a rubble base topped by huge concrete blocks – some 66 000 blocks, each weighing 5 or 10 tons, were cast for the purpose at St Mary's Holm. After the war, a road surface was created along the Barriers, thereby taking the A961 southwards.

Among the workers on the Barriers were Italian prisoners-of-war, whose 1000-strong camp was on the tiny island of Lamb Holm, and in their spare time they built and lovingly decorated a chapel dedicated to the Queen of Peace.

The basic structure is two Nissen huts cunningly joined end to end, but they were transformed to the design of Domenico Chiocchetti, who had been a church decorator before the war. The entrance is embellished with pinnacles and a bellcote, and the interior blazes with colour and pattern, all achieved largely with materials salvaged from the sea.

top: The concrete blocks of a Churchill Barrier
right: The Italian Chapel
far right: Inside the Italian Chapel

Some further reading

P D Anderson, *Black Patie: The Life and Times of Patrick Stewart, Earl of Orkney, Lord of Shetland* (Edinburgh 1992)

R J Berry and H N Firth (eds), *The People of Orkney* (Kirkwall 1986)

L Burgher, *Orkney: An Illustrated Architectural Guide* (Edinburgh 1991)

B E Crawford, *Scandinavian Scotland* (Leicester 1987)

B E Crawford (ed), *St. Magnus Cathedral and Orkney's Twelfth Century Renaissance* (Aberdeen 1988)

J L Davidson and A S Henshall, *The Chambered Cairns of Orkney* (Edinburgh 1989)

R Fawcett, *Scottish Medieval Churches* (Edinburgh 1985)

J Gifford, *Highland and Islands* (London 1992)

J W Hedges, *Tomb of the Eagles* (London 1984)

W S Hewison, *This Great Harbour – Scapa Flow* (Kirkwall 1985)

C Renfrew (ed), *The Prehistory of Orkney* (Edinburgh 1985)

A Ritchie, *Scotland BC* (Edinburgh 1988)

A Ritchie, *Picts* (Edinburgh 1989)

A Ritchie, *Orkney and Shetland* (Edinburgh 1993)

A Ritchie, *Viking Scotland* (London 1993)

A Ritchie, *Prehistoric Orkney* (London 1995)

J N G Ritchie, *Brochs of Scotland* (Aylesbury 1988)

W P L Thomson, *History of Orkney* (Edinburgh 1987)

Printed in Scotland for HMSO by CC No. 70343, Dd 293270, C75, 8/95